LinkedIn: 50 Powerful Strategies for Mastering Your Online Resume

Work for Your Dream Company!

Jonathan A. Eagle

D1551212

Introduction

LinkedIn is a social networking service which caters to the professional market. LinkedIn was founded in December 2002 and launched in May 2003. It's allure and power is so unquestionable that Microsoft, the largest technology company in the word has acquired LinkedIn for almost 30 **billion** dollars.

Since it's inception, LinkedIn has steadily grown and today has over 300 million people worldwide using it. Before we go any further, my assumption is that you have already at least got an account. If not, make one now and get comfortable with the layout and functions.

Many recruitment firms and employers both say that LinkedIn is their "go-to" for searching for potential candidates. If you're in the market for a job, or wish to develop your career - you simply cannot afford to not make use of this tool.

I hope this breakdown of strategies proves useful to you in your quest to work for your dream company! With the right mindset and know-how, there is no reason why this is not possible.

Table of Contents

21. *Describe what makes you valuable at your job.*

22. *Specify your accomplishments.*

23. *Strategically refine your collection of recommendations.*

24. *Share interesting articles and news items with your network.*

25. *Do your volunteer work.*

Chapter 4: Extend Your Profile

26. *Write and publish your own articles or eBooks.*

27. *Create a blog to accompany your profile.*

28. *Incorporate multimedia into your profile.*

29. *Create a custom URL for your profile.*

30. *Use LinkedIn plugins to integrate your website.*

31. *Limit your embellishments to the most essential.*

Chapter 5: Tell Your Story

32. *Express some of your values.*

33. *Talk about some of your experiences.*

34. *Talk about events, associations, and conferences that you have participated in.*

35. *Present yourself as a well-rounded person.*

36. *Share some interesting facts about yourself.*

37. *Capture the viewer's imagination with your summary.*

38. *Describe your future career plans.*

39. *Increase the credibility of your accomplishments with numbers.*

40. *Make it clear that you will move on the right opportunity.*

Chapter 1: Profile Essentials

When developing your LinkedIn profile, it is necessary to go beyond the basics. It is perhaps most important that you upload your resume; however, that is only the beginning. You must also complete your recent employment history and educational attainment. You want for your profile to demonstrate that you are a serious professional who has valuable contributions to make to your field. If you have a current profile, type your name into a search engine. Examine the search results and ask yourself what you liked and what you would prefer to have shown up. LinkedIn profiles are to be highly indexed on search engines, therefore your profile is more than an online resume it is how the online world sees you.

1. ***Establish a clear purpose for you profile.*** Not everybody has the same reason for being on LinkedIn. Generic profiles are often passed over, because they do not stand out in comparison with the more strategic profiles that are designed with clear intent. For example, people may align the contents of their profile with their purpose for being on LinkedIn, such as:
   - Someone actively seeking a new job might focus their profile around endorsements, certifications, and recommendations from colleagues and supervisors.
   - A passive job seeker might discuss their current roles and responsibilities on their job and discuss new challenges that they are interested in pursuing.

- A person looking to expand their network might focus their profile on discussing events going on in different places throughout their industry.
- A person looking to establish themselves as an influencer in their field might write and publish articles on the LinkedIn platform, post articles and research on their profile, and actively participate in groups.

When you design your LinkedIn profile around your central purpose, it more closely aligns you with those who are on the same path, either as fellow job seekers or those looking for potential employees.

2. *Use a flattering profile picture.* From a variety of photos, select the one that most accurately communicates the message that you want to portray. The image should be close up, displaying your shoulders and head. The image should be clearly focused and well lit. Your background should be simple and not distract from the primary focal point, which is your smile. It is not necessary to take a photo at your desk or even in your work environment. Many outstanding profile pictures are taken in comfortable surroundings, such as home or nature. Photos of you doing something active can also help to evoke the image of you blending in to someone's work setting. Just remember that it must clearly show your face in order for viewers to be able to connect with it. Your dress should be appropriate for your particular work setting. The goal of your profile

picture on LinkedIn is to convey professionalism, and humanity in a clear and attractive photograph.

3. ***Create a captivating headline.*** Your headline is one of the first things visitors notice when they view your profile. Create a memorable headline that is easy to find in the search results, using words related to your job. If you are seeking a new job, then it will not be particularly helpful for you to use your headline space to list your current place of employment and job title. The words that you use in your headline are important determinants of whether your profile appears in search results. Use the headline section to list your area of specialty, your value to employers, and what makes you so special. The more specific and targeted the words in your headline, the better your likely response. Whenever you switch your recent job role or employer, LinkedIn changes your headline to whatever your new title is. That of course will not help you attract job recruiters. Therefore, you should write a captivating custom headline to help distinguish you from all of the other job seekers.

4. ***Make your profile reader-friendly.*** A series of full paragraphs makes it hard to see the key information that recruiters look for in order to determine if you are right for a job with their company. Add a line between individual paragraphs. Highlight your achievements with bulleted lists to make them stand out. Be sparing with the number of words that you use. Readers are more likely to quickly glance at your profile

than they are to spend time mulling through your descriptions. Make sure that the most important information stands out and can be understood without further explanation.

5. **Use a LinkedIn email signature.** By placing a conspicuous link to your LinkedIn profile in your various email signatures, you will definitely get more viewers and connections. To do this:

   a. Save the following image to your computer:

   http://bit.ly/2d99ppd

   b. Log in to your LinkedIn profile, and copy your profile URL.
   c. Log in to your email, select "Options" and "Include Signature."
   d. If you already have an email signature, choose it. If you do not, select "New" and write the information that you would like.
   e. Insert your LinkedIn button image wherever you'd like.
   f. Right click on the button image and select "Insert Hyperlink."
   g. Finally, paste the URL to your LinkedIn profile URL in the hyperlink box, and click "Ok"
   h. At this point your signature is complete, and your button is live.

6. **Make it easy for people to contact you.** Be diligent about updating your email address, website, and social media profiles that you want to include. Many people neglect this, so you will have a competitive advantage.

7. ***Learn about your audience.*** Figure out who it is that you want to attract to your profile. Come up with a composite description of the ideal individual that you want to connect with. Perhaps they are recruiters or successful leaders in your profession. Determine what these individuals look for and incorporate those things into your profile.

8. ***Customize the look of your profile.*** Stand out visually. People should want to find out more about you just based on the attractiveness and layout of your profile. In order to do this, click and drag the various sections to rearrange them on your profile in a way that best accomplishes the goal you are trying to achieve. emphasizes in order to make a picture your background image:

   a. Place the cursor over "Profile" on your homepage.
   b. Click on "Edit Profile."
   c. Select the camera icon at the top of your profile.
   d. Choose an image file to upload from your computer.
   e. Click Save.

At this point you have created an outstanding profile. You know what it is that you want to achieve on LinkedIn, and you have customized your presentation to accomplish that goal. You have considered your target audience and included the type of information that they are looking for. Your profile is also visually appealing. This well-planned profile will open the door to further investigation of its creator. In the next section, we will discuss strategies for building the kind of network that you will need to further accomplish your objectives on LinkedIn.

Chapter 2: Build a Strong Network

9. ***Establish at least 50 connections.*** If you have fewer than 50 connections on your LinkedIn profile, it communicates to people that you are either not a well-known person or people are not interested in being associated with you. That kind of message is contrary to the image you want to project. On any social media platform, people make snap judgements based on the number of people who are associated with your account. This is particularly true of LinkedIn, where people consider not only quantity, but also quality of connections. Ideally, you want to have a target range of 50-200 connections. More than 150 brings into doubt the quality of your relationships with such a high number of people, and we already know what people think when they see fewer than fifty. In the beginning, the quality of your connections may consist of low to mid-range peers, who are all essentially in your same category. This will at least show that you are interested in associating with others, and they are likewise interested in being associated with you. Such a status opens the door for you to begin reach up into higher levels of your profession and connecting with higher-value individuals in your field.

10. ***Join relevant groups.*** Groups in LinkedIn are a valuable source of information and connections. Joining the right groups for you can help a great deal with finding jobs or accomplishing any other goal that you have for this site. Join select groups

in your profession or career field to demonstrate that you are engaged in your professional community. Use groups to easily connect with people and participate in important discussions about your industry. There are many different groups to select from. When considering which ones to join, try to select a few main groups that your associates and preferred recruiters belong to. Do your part to make useful contributions by contributing information and responding to other members' posts. Just avoid soliciting or trying to capitalize on relationships on the group platform. There is a time and place for everything; group discussions are for professional discussions, not for sales pitches. Save those for conversations that take place outside of the platform through email, phone calls, over coffee, or any other place outside of the group forum. Active membership in LinkedIn groups is a form of social proof and validation. Take advantage to display your value as a team player and occasional leader through your interactions within your few, select groups. Members will see, take note, and discuss the most valuable contributors.

11. ***Become a member of your university alumni group.*** It can be very helpful to stay in touch with your alma mater. Associations based on alumni affiliations can create instant connections between people on a meaningful level. Try to keep abreast of developments and opportunities among your alumni community. Even when an opportunity does not pertain to you, try to see if you can help someone else out.

12. ***Use discretion when adding people that you do not know.*** In order to grow your network, you will definitely need to connect with strangers. When doing so, send them a short message about why you are adding them. If too many people reject your request and say they don't know you, LinkedIn will shut down your profile. Additionally, potential employers who know them may ask about you, and you don't want them to respond by saying that you are just some random stranger who added them. You want them to know why you added them and to be able to reference a couple of meaningful interactions that you've had with them after making your connection.

13. ***Follow high-quality people in your field.*** The quality of your network is important in LinkedIn. Whom you are connected with is more important than the number of connections. Use the platform to expand beyond your local network. Follow leaders and successful peers in your career field. When you follow such people, you will have greater access to information, news, and advice that can benefit you. By interacting with such people, you can establish collegiality and eventually develop relationships from which opportunities may arise.

14. ***Form deeper connections with your workmates.*** Relationships at work can get so focused on tasks at hand that colleagues do not get much opportunity to share thoughts on the bigger picture. LinkedIn provides a great opportunity to

cultivate this aspect of your working relationships, without having to spend additional time at a meeting. The things that you post and articles you share may help your work team to better understand your perspective and recognize your value to the team.

15. ***Get to know coworkers outside of your department.*** It can be very helpful to use LinkedIn to get to know coworkers that you do not actually interact with at work. This can be of great value to you, because on some level your work intersects with their work. You never know if someone on the other side of the building can be instrumental in helping you accomplish your goals. Likewise, be open to ways that you can be of assistance to them from your department. The fact that you have productive relationships with such a variety of people could come in handy during promotional opportunities.

16. ***Establish a presence in your network.*** When you establish your network, it is important to establish and maintain a presence. Obviously, you do not want to be a nuisance, constantly posting things that have no value for others. However, you want to post and share regularly enough that people expect to see contributions from you. Such contributions may include new items, articles, research, workplace humor, personal observations, etc. A recruiter might contact a random person in your network to solicit feedback about you, so you want to make sure that everyone in your network knows who you are and can honestly say something positive about you.

Business is highly social, and the quality of your LinkedIn network attests to whether or not you are the type of person that people feel comfortable bringing into their social business world. Going to work every day without interacting with the people around you is not conducive to getting ahead on your job; neither is it conducive to getting ahead through LinkedIn. Fortunately, social media platforms such as this have made it simple to connect with people from every aspect of our careers. Simple acts, such as commenting, liking, and sharing are all great ways to establish a rapport with someone new, and maintain contact with former coworkers. Using LinkedIn's mobile app can help you to access the news and events that are trending among your network, and directly communicate with people in your network, including clients and potential employers, effortlessly.

17. ***Get references from your current job.***
When applying for a new job opportunity, you have to provide letters of reference. Why wait until that time to start asking people? LinkedIn provides a platform for you to include such references as part of your profile. Contact former supervisors and get some recommendation letters posted for everyone to see. You could even ask for some references from current employers. This is not a necessity, and if you feel uncomfortable asking, then you may want to forgo that opportunity. It could be awkward for a current employer to put in writing that you are awesome, when frankly there is no telling what the future

holds. You could mitigate this, however, by asking them to acknowledge the wonderful things they said about you in your latest employee evaluation. That way they are not going out on a limb, so to speak, with their comments. You could also solicit coworkers to give you references based on specific projects that you worked on together or assistance that you have given them.

18. **Invite people to add you to their networks.** Make it clear in your profile that you are very open to meeting new people and supporting others in their goals. A simple tagline that lets viewers know that you are interested in collaborating on projects, learning what they have to teach, and sharing the benefits of your experience will help people to feel comfortable reaching out to you and including you in their network.

This section discussed strategies for growing and strengthening the quality of your network. It is important to demonstrate social value by having at least 50 professional connections in your network. You eventually want to build your network up in number, but only with people that you have authentic connections with, either through real-life experience or through meaningful interactions on LinkedIn. You also want to cultivate your network to include high-value individuals. Due to the social nature of business, others will form preconceptions of you based on the quality of your network. Use this to your advantage. The following section discusses ways in which you can communicate your value as a professional by the things you include on your profile.

Chapter 3: Demonstrate Your Value

It can be challenging enough for you to be discovered online by a recruiter. When one does come across your profile, you need for them to immediately recognize your value. It is not likely that a busy executive is going to spend a great amount of time reading your profile and calculating your value, relative to the countless other profiles that they are skimming. If you want others to know your value, you have to spell it out for them. Your profile should be organized and written in such a way that your value statements are the first thing a viewer sees. This chapter discusses specific tips for accomplishing this important task.

19. ***Be specific about your education.*** Simply stating the type of degree that you received a particular university might be good enough if you graduated from Harvard. For everyone else, it is helpful to elaborate on more specific learning experiences and training that you received along the way. Highlight particular areas in your field of study in which you excelled; discuss interesting projects that you worked on; point out a well-known professor that you studied under. Make sure that your education section makes an impression on your visitors.

20. ***Present your certifications and endorsements.*** Listing your professional endorsements is an efficient way to display your

skills. However, listing excess endorsements obscures the most important ones. Maintain an updated list of your skills, and leave out those that are from several years ago or are common among everyone. For example, basic MS Office productivity skills are so common, that they are not always worth listing. If you do not have a long list, include them; but if you have been certified in a variety of specialty areas, highlight those alone. Your certificates and endorsements should give the impression that you are on the cutting edge of what is happening in your industry. If your list looks a little dated to you, then get busy on some new endorsements, so that you can add them to your profile.

21. ***Describe what makes you valuable at your job.*** When discussing your roles and responsibilities at work, do not make a list of things that you are required to do. Instead, describe how you make valuable contributions to your organization. An easy way to accomplish this is to write in active, 1st person voice. For example, replace "Provide customer support" with "I ensure that customer needs are met through direct support." Describe things that you provide that help your organization to be successful, and do not beat around the bush. Explicitly state such things as, "My advanced knowledge of MS Excel enables me to automate tasks for our team, which makes us more productive." You LinkedIn profile is not the place for modesty. Consider that you are stating concrete and verifiable facts, which are far different from inflated opinions of yourself.

22. **Specify your accomplishments.** Industry recruiters skim through thousands of profiles searching for high performing individuals. They do not have time to read every line of the profiles they come across. In order to get your profile noticed, a viewer should be able to see your accomplishments at a glance. Your accomplishments should be simply stated and conspicuously displayed. You can do this by making them one-line bullet points, or using bold letters, or both. Once someone temporarily stops their search to look deeper into these accomplishments, they should be able to see the story behind each one located conveniently below the highlighted accomplishment, in a sparse descriptive statement. Build your profile around the fact that you have a proven record of high performance, using supporting evidence, such as statistics, awards, and commendations.

23. **Strategically refine your collection of recommendations.** When you are considering a purchase or a destination you would like to travel to, you are able to conveniently read the associated reviews. If for some reason a product or service does not have any reviews, you may likely be inclined to bypass it for one that does. Even if the other product does not have all perfect reviews. Like all consumers, recruiters are not likely place their trust in a product that no one has reviewed. Earlier in this book, we discussed the importance of gathering recommendations from supervisors and colleagues. Once you have received a sufficient number of recommendations, you should consider

that a recruiter is unlikely to read through all of them. Rather that overload your profile with a mixture of recommendations that include those from high and low-level professionals, as well as many that repeat the same basic information, you should select a few recommendations that discuss various aspects of your value. For example, even if a baseball player has a high batting average, coaches will still want to know other information, perhaps about their fielding skills or their work ethic. View your recommendations as a composite description of you as a worker. One recommendation that highlights your interpersonal skills is sufficient; there is no need to include 3 more. Doing so increases the risk of a recruiter reading 2 or 3 letters about your people skills and missing the one about your perfect attendance record or leadership ability.

When requesting recommendation letters, ask different people to discuss specific aspects of you as an employee. That will help to ensure that you have sufficient variety. Let them know that they can keep their letters brief and to the point. Your colleagues need not spend more than a few minutes to complete the type of recommendation that you need for your profile. Also, your recommendations do not have to be full summations of you as a worker; they can be brief commendations on specific tasks or projects.

24. ***Share interesting articles and news items with your network.*** As an involved member of your professional community, you should be a reliable source of useful information. You will

know that you have successfully accomplished this when people in your network begin to ask you about events and news in your industry; that means they respect you as a source of information and also expect you to be consistent with your information. In order to be able to consistently share useful and interesting information, you will need to find some reliable sources of your own. All major industries have professional trade magazines, academic journals, special interest groups, and reliable news sources. You can set Google Alerts to notify you when news items are published concerning your specific topics. You can also link your blog, website, or email to RSS feeds from relevant blogs and websites. That will provide a convenient source of information to skim through and select items that your network will appreciate. When you find an item to share, make sure that you actually read it first. Doing so will provide a layer of quality control (you can learn if the article is a dud before you send it out), and you will be able to participate in discussions that may ensue. One word of caution: be sparing with the items that you share. A few articles per week is sufficient. If you post too much, you will be considered a nuisance by your network. Only share the most interesting and relative pieces.

25. ***Do your volunteer work.*** One limitation with being an employee is that your job responsibilities do not always reflect your range of skills and abilities. If you have more to offer than is being utilized in your current position (which might be why you are looking for a better job) then consider

donating a few hours a month or a week to volunteering your skills to a worthy cause. Nonprofits, religious organizations, schools, and even individuals can always benefit from trained professionals lending a helping hand. This not only benefits the people for whom you are volunteering; it also helps you to demonstrate your skills. Do not be afraid to ask for a letter of recommendation from those whom you assist. Such letters add to your current list of recommendations and also verify the volunteer work that you have done.

Chapter 4: Extend Your Profile

26. ***Write and publish your own articles or eBooks.*** LinkedIn allows users to write and publish articles on the platform. Write brief, well-constructed articles about issues that are related to your related field. Conduct an analysis of an important trends, and discuss the importance of your findings. This gives you an opportunity to participate in the bigger discussions, display your talents, and be perceived in a leadership role. The fact that you are the author of the article is sufficient to get you noticed, so it is not necessary to write a piece that is specifically about you or would only be interesting to your coworkers. Nobody is inclined to read someone's self-congratulatory essay. To select a topic, research trending topics in your network. Find our something that the majority seems to be interested in learning about or discussing, and find a new angle from which to add to the topic. For example, if the slumping economy is threatening layoffs in your industry, and everyone is talking about it, write a short piece wherein you summarize what leading authorities are predicting for the upcoming year. Once you have finished your article, have people proofread and critique it. You want to be confident that anyone who reads it online knows that it was written by a knowledgeable and competent professional in the industry. Do not overdo it with jargon and fancy words; you want to impress people with your content, not your flashy style. Publishing occasional articles will let colleagues and recruiters

know that you have the ability to communicate well in writing and the confidence to share your professional views with others.

27. ***Create a blog to accompany your profile.*** It is beneficial for you to have a professional blog online that extends beyond what you have on LinkedIn. Having a blog affords you the freedom to publish as much content as you want. It is also an appropriate platform to write about things that are focused on you. Unlike the items that you share on your LinkedIn feed, which need to appeal to a mass audience, your blog can be all about you. This is because your blog posts do not go out to anyone unless they subscribe to it. For those who come across your profile and would like to know more about you, they can click the link to your blog and learn enough to feel as though they know you. When a recruiter forms such a familiar perception of you, it skyrockets you past all of the other one dimensional prospects that they are considering. If you are comfortable with writing, then have at it. If you are not very comfortable with writing enough content to fill out a blog, then feature writing and articles from others and provide brief commentary and reviews.

28. ***Incorporate multimedia into your profile.*** Bring your profile to life by providing more than static pictures and text. Include work samples, eBooks, videos, slideshows, podcasts, and other media that either comes from your work experience or that you create specifically for your profile. This will convert your digital resume into a

multimedia portfolio, wherein viewers can learn about you through a rich experience. Doing this is a way of creating a brand for your professional image. To add media:

    a. Select "Edit profile,"
    b. Go down to the Summary section,
    c. Select the box symbol,
    d. Click "add file,"
    e. Upload your media.

29. ***Create a custom URL for your profile.***
Instead of using the default profile URL that looks like: http://linkedin.com/pub/first-lastsfljier9fgjfg8. Shorten your profile URL to include just your first name and last name (e.g., https://www.linkedin.com/in/FirstNameLastNam e). To do this:
- Go to your profile.
- Select "Edit Profile."
- Select "Edit" below your profile picture.
- Enter your new URL.

If your first name and last name is not available, add your middle initial or name (e.g., FirstNameMiddleInitialLastName).

30. *Use LinkedIn plugins to integrate your website.* If you have a relevant website that you use for business, there are a variety of plugins that you can use to integrate LinkedIn with your website. Some examples include:

a. WP LinkedIn

This plugin allows you to display elements of your profile directly on your website. This includes your list of recommendations and you network updates.

b. LinkedIn SC
This plugin allows you to display discreet elements of your profile on your website.

c. LinkedIn Auto Publish
This plugin automatically publishes your blog posts to your LinkedIn profile.

d. FP LinkedIn Profile
This plugin presents a scaled down version of your LinkedIn profile on your website as a customizable summary card.

e. LinkedIn Profile Synchronizer Tool
This plugin allows people to give you recommendations from the WordPress commenting tool. These recommendations are automatically published to your profile.

31. ***Limit your embellishments to the most essential.*** There are many things that you can do to enhance your profile. However, it is not necessary to do all of them at once. The purpose is to use enhancements to draw attention to your profile and highlight your most important elements. If you include too many bells and whistles, then it will distract your viewers from the main focal points. Experiment with all of the available ways to accentuate your profile, and

narrow them down to 2 or 3 that best accomplish your purpose.

This chapter discussed a variety of ways in which you can enhance and extend your LinkedIn profile. There is only so much that you can communicate with an image and text. With all of the users on LinkedIn, it is helpful to add multimedia to draw in viewers and highlight the most important parts of your profile. By publishing material, incorporating a blog, and embedding LinkedIn plugins into your website, you give colleagues and prospective employers an opportunity to get to know you on a much deeper level.

Chapter 5: Tell Your Story

This chapter discusses ways in which you can make a more meaningful impression on your network and potential employers by providing a glimpse into your personal life.

32. ***Express some of your values.*** Although the business world may seem primarily concerned with your utility as a worker, the social nature of business makes your personal characteristics important as well. Although it may not be advisable to tell your deepest secrets to the general work force, it does not hurt to express some aspects of your personal values. By doing this, your new contacts and connection will be able to relate to you on a human level. This also helps you to stand out among all of the other individuals who present themselves as little more than a big smile and collection of industry buzz words.

33. ***Talk about some of your experiences.*** Experience is a wonderful teacher, and you can benefit from sharing some of your experiences on your profile. The experiences that you share should tie in to how you became the great professional that you are today. An experience that you share may illustrate how you came to see the importance of what you do. A different experience might describe how you learned from a failure how to become persistent and believe in yourself. Personal experiences are relatable to everyone. Use your discretion when sharing experiences; you do not want to come off like a hero and seem

disingenuous, but you also want to refrain from making yourself look like a fool. Keep your experiences relatable, and relate them to how you became a better professional as a result.

34. ***Talk about events, associations, and conferences that you have participated in.***
You can further establish yourself as a mover and shaker inside of your industry by mentioning your participation in professional associations and events. It communicates that you are part of the bigger picture in your career field and have the potential to become a leader in your profession. It is not necessary to elaborate extensively on this, because you must conserve the majority of your space to highlight your accomplishments. However, this can nicely complement the achievements that you have made in the day to day work environments.

35. ***Present yourself as a well-rounded person.***
At this point, you have clearly established your level of immersion in your career and the honors you have earned along the way. There is now a little room for you to mention some of your personal interests and hobbies. When selecting which things you would like to share, try not to be generic. I like to go to church, read, and exercise is not exactly attention grabbing. You should mention things that make you stand out a little more. What types of books do you like to read, or who is your favorite author? What type of exercises to you like to do, and what current goals are you working toward? What activities have you

participated in with your church? Think along those lines, so that people have something to remember you by.

36. ***Share some interesting facts about yourself.*** This can be a small, separate section in which you share a few fun facts about yourself. In this case, it is acceptable to include random information that is not related to your professional identity. Perhaps you met somebody famous, or participated in some interesting event. Maybe you are allergic to cats, or you acted the part of a villain in a school play. A small section entitled "Interesting Facts about Me" is certain to draw attention and generate interest in you.

37. ***Capture the viewer's imagination with your summary.*** The summary section is very important for telling the story of your career. Not every career occurs in a straight and logical path. In fact, some of the most successful careers are characterized by unexpected twists and turns. You do not have a lot of space to summarize your story, so be conservative with your words and explain your career path in a way that makes sense and leaves no unanswered questions. If a recruiter cannot make sense of your summary or notices inexplicable gaps, chances are you will never get the opportunity to explain in person. Write, rewrite, and refine your summary until it is concise and crystal clear.

38. ***Describe your future career plans.*** You are at the point in your profile where a viewer knows your story and is aware of all that you bring to your career field. In this section (which should be

at the end of your summary) you should describe how you see yourself in the future of your career. It is helpful in this case to use active language, wherein you describe the kinds of things you are making happen and the legacy that you are building. It is more interesting for you to describe your impact in the future of your career than the rewards you hope to receive.

39. ***Increase the credibility of your accomplishments with numbers.*** Just like a picture speaks volumes, so do well presented numbers. When describing your accomplishments, try to quantify them with numbers as much as possible. If it is applicable, consider adding charts, graphs, or infographics. This visual representations of numbers are particularly eye catching and relay the level of impact and achievement that your text is describing. Doing this will give you a distinct advantage in the online world.

40. ***Make it clear that you will move on the right opportunity.*** If you are ready and willing to begin working at a new place of employment, definitely say so. You do not want to leave any room for doubt when colleagues and recruiters glance at your profile. Recruiters are looking for individuals who are ready to go, and colleagues will think about you when they come across available opportunities. Simply make a subtle statement to the effect that you are willing to relocate for an opportunity in which you can use your experience and skills to make a meaningful impact.

41. ***Talk about a specific area of specialty in your field.*** In your summary, mention a specialty that you either have in your profession, or one that you are cultivating. Although you want to present yourself as a well-rounded employee in general, you should select one particular area to distinguish as your specialty. Such a specialty does not have to be an established category in your profession (especially if it requires a certification). It can be a special talent that you integrate into your job. Such talents can be bilingualism, people skills, technology skills, research, data analysis, or anything else that you believe adds value to what you do.

42. ***Use privacy settings to limit what your current employer can see.*** It is not always wise to let your employer know that you are actively seeking employment elsewhere. Use the built in privacy settings to control who can see certain parts of your profile information. For obvious reasons you should be selective about what anyone in your current place of employment has access to.

This chapter presented some tips on helping viewers to identify with you as a complete person by revealing small bits of information about yourself beyond the scope of your professional accomplishments. It is beneficial to show people in your network that you are more than a worker and have personality and values that you bring to your profession.

Chapter 6: Stay Current

It is important to keep your profile on all forms of social media, but none so important as LinkedIn. On this platform being current is indicative of one's professionalism and seriousness about connecting with colleagues and recruiters. In this chapter, we will discuss strategies for maintaining a current and professional profile.

43. ***Keep your contact information up to date.*** It is important that you provide people with multiple ways to get in touch with you. It is equally important that you keep these email addresses, profile links, websites, blogs, phone numbers, and anything else that you have listed current. If a recruiter reaches out to you and is unable to connect, or if they leave a message on a site link that you do not regularly check, it is not likely that they will keep trying to get in touch with you. It is not necessary to have a plethora of ways to contact you, so limit your contact information to those that you check on a regular basis, and keep those up to date.

44. ***Maintain your profile regularly.*** Some elements of your profile do not need to be updated often, such as your profile picture or your phone number. That, however, does not mean that is alright to leave your profile unattended. Check your profile regularly for messages. Also keep your posts current. A profile wherein the latest post was months ago appears to be out of date to the casual observer. Whether or not you are interested in

being active in your network, you should visit your profile regularly and update elements of your status. That way viewers will know that you are active.

45. **Discuss your most recent duties, responsibilities, and projects.** Although your job description may not change very often, the specific tasks that you work on change frequently. Update these in your profile. You may include a small section labeled, "Current Responsibilities" and keep that current with the things that you are working on and our latest successes and accomplishments. This shows that you are diligent with your profile, and it gives people a reason to check in on you.

46. **Complete the Current Job Entry, even if you are between jobs.** The majority of recruiters only look at your current job title in their search for prospects. This prevents them from wasting time reading through numerous profiles that used to fit their criterion years ago. If you are currently between jobs, fill that section out with the type of job that you are currently seeking, and fill out the Company box with something like, "Independent." This will keep you in the running, and you can explain that you were laid off or that your company relocated or whatever else may have happened in your complete profile section.

47. **Be strategic with your updates.** As mentioned earlier, you should be sparing with your number of updates per week, 3-4 is plenty.

You should also be strategic with the types of things that you share. In addition to sharing research, interesting articles, and your own written material, you should include congratulations to colleagues who have made achievements, condolences to those going through a difficult time, and other various ways to show that you have genuine interest in your network. When a viewer looks at your recent posts, they should see a variety of interests expressed around the central topic of your career field.

This chapter discussed the importance of maintaining a current and professional profile. It is important to let people know that you are active on the site. You should only include contact information to things that you check daily. Your updates should be regular and reflect a variety of interests that you have around your career field. The next chapter discusses the importance of language on LinkedIn.

Chapter 7: The Importance of Language

LinkedIn is a platform on which most of your presentation is in written format. It is therefore important to consider the language that you use. This chapter discusses some tips for benefitting from the use of specific language on LinkedIn.

48. ***Include your language proficiencies.*** If you speak a second language, you definitely want to highlight that. If you do not, you should definitely consider learning one. There are a variety of free, online programs that can help you to become proficient in another language on your own time and at your own pace. Get started with one and indicated that you are developing proficiency in that particular language. Consider a second language like computer proficiency; it is no longer an option.

49. ***Avoid using generic words, phrases, and industry jargon.*** The written language throughout your profile should be in simple and effective language. The problem with industry jargon is that is means different things to different people. It is also easily dated. Hot buzz words from 2 years ago may seem out of place today. When you take the time to carefully write personal statements, you do not want to have to update them every time trends change. Write in classic, timeless style throughout your profile.

50. ***Use key words from employers' job descriptions.*** Examine the wording in job descriptions that you are seeking to attain. When you find words that come up repeatedly, consider them to be "key" words. Use these key words throughout the text in your profile and especially in your heading. What this will do is rank you high in the search engine when recruiters look for candidates for the jobs that you want. Once the read your profile, those words will resonate with them. This combined with your highlighted accomplishments, multimedia files, links to your additional written content, and your snippets of personal life are certain to place you near the top of their list for people to contact.

This chapter discussed the importance of language in your profile. When writing descriptions in the various sections, use clear, simple, and timeless language. Utilize key words from the job descriptions that you desire to attain. Also highlight the second language that you are fluent in, or the language in which you are working towards fluency.

Conclusion

I would like to thank you once again for your purchase of this book. By utilizing the strategies discussed, I sincerely hope that you have already landed your dream job. If you are yet to receive your most sought-after opportunity, fear not. Employment search can be a long and treacherous journey, but keep the faith. Constantly analyze your profile and the direction of your career within your current job. It may be that you might need to accept a job as a "stepping-stone" to the job that you really want.

Made in the USA
Charleston, SC
15 November 2016